# IAPP CIPP-US Questions & Dumps

Exam Prep Questions for CIPP-US updated version with References

Authored By: Maxim Books

MAXIM BOOKS

## Copyright Notice © 2023 – Maxim Books

Protected by copyright law. No piece of this distribution might be repeated, distributed, or sent in any structure or using any and all means, including copying, recording, or other electronic or robotized strategies, without the earlier composed assent of the distributor, with the exception of brief citations exemplified in basic audits and certain other noncommercial purposes allowed by intellectual property owner.

## About Maxim Books:

Maxim Books is a book publishing company incorporated in Dallas, Texas, USA, a place that is accessible both on the web and locally, which releases the force of education substances, Certifications guidebooks, poetry, and numerous other book genres. We make it simple for authors and writers to get their books planned, distributed, marketed, and sell expertly on an international scale with digital book + Print conveyance. Maxim Books was established in 2018 and expanding its business in more countries

Note: Answers of the questions are at the end of the book

## QUESTION 1

What is a **legal** document approved by a judge that formalizes an agreement between a governmental agency and an adverse party called?

A. A consent decree
B. *Stare decisis* decree
C. A judgment rider
D. Common law judgment

## QUESTION 2

Read this notice:

*Our website uses cookies. Cookies allow us to identify the computer or device you're using to access the site, but they don't identify you personally. For instructions on setting your Web browser to refuse cookies, click* here.

What type of legal choice does not notice provide?

A. Mandatory
B. Implied consent
C. Opt-in
D. Opt-out

## QUESTION 3
SCENARIO
Please use the following to answer the next question:

Cheryl is the sole owner of Fitness Coach, Inc., a medium-sized company that helps individuals realize their physical fitness goals through classes, individual instruction, and access to an extensive indoor gym. She has owned the company for ten years and has always been concerned about protecting customer's privacy while maintaining the highest level of service. She is proud that she has built long-lasting customer relationships.

Although Cheryl and her staff have tried to make privacy protection a priority, the company has no formal privacy policy. So Cheryl hired Janice, a privacy professional, to help her develop one.

After an initial assessment, Janice created a first of a new policy. Cheryl read through the draft and was concerned about the many changes the policy would bring throughout the company. For example, the draft policy stipulates that a customer's personal information can only be held for one year after paying for a service such as a session with personal trainer. It also promises that customer information will not be shared with third parties without the written consent of the customer. The wording of these rules worry Cheryl since stored personal information often helps her company to serve her customers, even if there are long pauses between their visits. In addition, there are some third parties that provide crucial services, such as aerobics instructors who teach classes on a contract basis. Having access to customer files and understanding the fitness levels of their students helps instructors to organize their classes.

Janice understood Cheryl's concerns and was already formulating some ideas for revision. She tried to put Cheryl at ease by pointing out that customer data can still be kept, but that it should be classified according to levels of sensitivity. However, Cheryl was skeptical. It seemed that classifying data and treating each type differently would cause undue difficulties in the company's day-to-day operations. Cheryl wants one simple data storage and access system that any employee can access if needed.

Even though the privacy policy was only a draft, she was beginning to see that changes within her company were going to be necessary. She told Janice that she would be more comfortable with implementing the new policy gradually over a period of several months, one department at a time. She was also interested in a layered approach by creating documents listing applicable parts of the new policy for each department.

What is the **best** reason for Cheryl to follow Janice's suggestion about classifying customer data?

A. It will help employees stay better organized
B. It will help the company meet a federal mandate
C. It will increase the security of customers' personal information (PI)
D. It will prevent the company from collecting too much personal information (PI)

### QUESTION 4
SCENARIO
Please use the following to answer the next question:

Cheryl is the sole owner of Fitness Coach, Inc., a medium-sized company that helps individuals realize their physical fitness goals through classes, individual instruction, and access to an extensive indoor gym. She has owned the company for ten years and has always been concerned about protecting customer's privacy while maintaining the highest level of service. She is proud that she has built long-lasting customer relationships.

Although Cheryl and her staff have tried to make privacy protection a priority, the company has no formal privacy policy. So Cheryl hired Janice, a privacy professional, to help her develop one.

After an initial assessment, Janice created a first of a new policy. Cheryl read through the draft and was concerned about the many changes the policy would bring throughout the company. For example, the draft policy stipulates that a customer's personal information can only be held for one year after paying for a service such as a session with personal trainer. It also promises that customer information will not be shared with third parties without the written consent of the customer. The wording of these rules worry Cheryl since stored personal information often helps her company to serve her customers, even if there are long pauses between their visits. In addition, there are some third parties that provide crucial services, such as aerobics instructors who teach classes on a contract basis. Having access to customer files and understanding the fitness levels of their students helps instructors to organize their classes.

Janice understood Cheryl's concerns and was already formulating some ideas for revision. She tried to put Cheryl at ease by pointing out that customer data can still be kept, but that it should be classified according to levels of sensitivity. However, Cheryl was skeptical. It seemed that classifying data and treating each type differently would cause undue difficulties in the company's day-to-day operations. Cheryl wants one simple data storage and access system that any employee can access if needed.

Even though the privacy policy was only a draft, she was beginning to see that changes within her company were going to be necessary. She told Janice that she would be more comfortable with implementing the new policy gradually over a period of several months, one department at a time. She was also interested in a layered approach by creating documents listing applicable parts of the new policy for each department.


What is the **main** problem with Cheryl's suggested method of communicating the new privacy policy?

A. The policy would not be considered valid if not communicated in full.
B. The policy might not be implemented consistency across departments.
C. Employees would not be comfortable with a policy that is

put into action over time.
Employees might not understand how the documents relate to the policy as a whole.

**QUESTION 5**
SCENARIO
Please use the following to answer the next question:

Cheryl is the sole owner of Fitness Coach, Inc., a medium-sized company that helps individuals realize their physical fitness goals through classes, individual instruction, and access to an extensive indoor gym. She has owned the company for ten years and has always been concerned about protecting customer's privacy while maintaining the highest level of service. She is proud that she has built long-lasting customer relationships.

Although Cheryl and her staff have tried to make privacy protection a priority, the company has no formal privacy policy. So Cheryl hired Janice, a privacy professional, to help her develop one.

After an initial assessment, Janice created a first of a new policy. Cheryl read through the draft and was concerned about the many changes the policy would bring throughout the company. For example, the draft policy stipulates that a customer's personal information can only be held for one year after paying for a service such as a session with personal trainer. It also promises that customer information will not be shared with third parties without the written consent of the customer. The wording of these rules worry Cheryl since stored personal information often helps her company to serve her customers, even if there are long pauses between their visits. In addition, there are some third parties that provide crucial services, such as aerobics instructors who teach classes on a contract basis. Having access to customer files and understanding the fitness levels of their students helps instructors to organize their classes.

Janice understood Cheryl's concerns and was already formulating some ideas for revision. She tried to put Cheryl at ease by pointing out that customer data can still be kept, but that it should be classified according to levels of sensitivity. However, Cheryl was skeptical. It seemed that classifying data and treating each type differently would cause undue difficulties in the company's day-to-day operations. Cheryl wants one simple data storage and access system that any employee can access if needed.

Even though the privacy policy was only a draft, she was beginning to see that changes within her company were going to be necessary. She told Janice that she would be more comfortable with implementing the new policy gradually over a period of several months, one department at a time. She was also interested in a layered approach by creating documents listing applicable parts of the new policy for each department.

Based on the scenario, which of the following would have helped Janice to better meet the company's needs?

A. Creating a more comprehensive plan for implementing a new policy
B. Spending more time understanding the company's information goals
C. Explaining the importance of transparency in implementing a new policy
Removing the financial burden of the company's employee training program

**QUESTION 6**
What is the **main** purpose of the Global Privacy Enforcement Network?

A. To promote universal cooperation among privacy

authorities
B. To investigate allegations of privacy violations internationally
C. To protect the interests of privacy consumer groups worldwide
D. To arbitrate disputes between countries over jurisdiction for privacy laws

## QUESTION 7

In 2014, Google was alleged to have violated the Family Educational Rights and Privacy Act (FERPA) through its Apps for Education suite of tools. For what specific practice did students sue the company?

A. Scanning emails sent to and received by students
B. Making student education records publicly available
C. Relying on verbal consent for a disclosure of education records
D. Disclosing education records without obtaining required consent

## QUESTION 8

An organization self-certified under Privacy Shield must, upon request by an individual, do what?

A. Suspend the use of all personal information collected by the organization to fulfill its original purpose.
B. Provide the identities of third parties with whom the organization shares personal information.
C. Provide the identities of third and fourth parties that may potentially receive personal information.
D. Identify all personal information disclosed during a criminal investigation.

## QUESTION 9
SCENARIO
Please use the following to answer the next question:

A US-based startup company is selling a new gaming application. One day, the CEO of the company receives an urgent letter from a prominent EU-based retail partner. Triggered by an unresolved complaint lodged by an EU resident, the letter describes an ongoing investigation by a supervisory authority into the retailer's data handling practices.

The complainant accuses the retailer of improperly disclosing her personal data, without consent, to parties in the United States. Further, the complainant accuses the EU-based retailer of failing to respond to her withdrawal of consent and request for erasure of her personal data. Your organization, the US-based startup company, was never informed of this request for erasure by the EU-based retail partner. The supervisory authority investigating the complaint has threatened the suspension of data flows if the parties involved do not cooperate with the investigation. The letter closes with an urgent request: "Please act immediately by identifying all personal data received from our company."

This is an important partnership. Company executives know that its biggest fans come from Western Europe; and this retailer is primarily responsible for the startup's rapid market penetration.

As the Company's data privacy leader, you are sensitive to the criticality of the relationship with the retailer.

At this stage of the investigation, what should the data privacy leader review first?

A. Available data flow diagrams
B. The text of the original complaint

C. The company's data privacy policies
Prevailing regulation on this subject

## QUESTION 10

A large online bookseller decides to contract with a vendor to manage Personal Information (PI). What is the **least** important factor for the company to consider when selecting the vendor?

A. The vendor's reputation
B. The vendor's financial health
C. The vendor's employee retention rates
D. The vendor's employee training program

## QUESTION 11

All of the following are tasks in the "Discover" phase of building an information management program EXCEPT?

A. Facilitating participation across departments and levels
B. Developing a process for review and update of privacy policies
C. Deciding how aggressive to be in the use of personal information
D. Understanding the laws that regulate a company's collection of information

## QUESTION 12

If an organization certified under Privacy Shield wants to transfer personal data to a third party acting as an agent, the organization must ensure the third party does all of the following EXCEPT?

A. Uses the transferred data for limited purposes

B. Provides the same level of privacy protection as the organization
C. Notifies the organization if it can no longer meet its requirements for proper data handling
D. Enters a contract with the organization that states the third party will process data according to the consent agreement

## QUESTION 13
SCENARIO
Please use the following to answer the next question:

Matt went into his son's bedroom one evening and found him stretched out on his bed typing on his laptop. "Doing your network?" Matt asked hopefully.
"No," the boy said. "I'm filling out a survey."

Matt looked over his son's shoulder at his computer screen. "What kind of survey?" "It's asking questions about my opinions."
"Let me see," Matt said, and began reading the list of questions that his son had already answered. "It's asking your opinions about the government and citizenship. That's a little odd. You're only ten."

Matt wondered how the web link to the survey had ended up in his son's email inbox. Thinking the message might have been sent to his son by mistake he opened it and read it. It had come from an entity called the Leadership Project, and the content and the graphics indicated that it was intended for children. As Matt read further he learned that kids who took the survey were automatically registered in a contest to win the first book in a series about famous leaders.

To Matt, this clearly seemed like a marketing ploy to solicit goods and services to children. He asked his son if he had been prompted to give information about himself in order to take the survey. His son told him he had been asked to give his name, address, telephone number, and date of birth, and to answer questions about his favorite games and toys.

Matt was concerned. He doubted if it was legal for the marketer to collect information from his son in the way that it was. Then he noticed several other commercial

emails from marketers advertising products for children in his son's inbox, and he decided it was time to report the incident to the proper authorities.

Based on the incident, the FTC's enforcement actions against the marketer would **most likely** include what violation?

A. Intruding upon the privacy of a family with young children.
B. Collecting information from a child under the age of thirteen.
C. Failing to notify of a breach of children's private information.
D. Disregarding the privacy policy of the children's marketing industry.

## QUESTION 14
What important action should a health care provider take if the she wants to qualify for funds under the Health Information Technology for Economic and Clinical Health Act (HITECH)?

A. Make electronic health records (EHRs) part of regular care
B. Bill the majority of patients electronically for their health care
C. Send health information and appointment reminders to patients electronically
D. Keep electronic updates about the Health Insurance

Portability and Accountability Act

**QUESTION 15**
A covered entity suffers a ransomware attack that affects the personal health information (PHI) of more than 500 individuals. According to Federal law under HIPAA, which of the following would the covered entity **NOT** have to report the breach to?

A. Department of Health and Human Services
B. The affected individuals
C. The local media
D. Medical providers

**QUESTION 16**
Who has rulemaking authority for the Fair Credit Reporting Act (FCRA) and the Fair and Accurate Credit Transactions Act (FACTA)?

A. State Attorneys General
B. The Federal Trade Commission
C. The Department of Commerce
D. The Consumer Financial Protection Bureau

**QUESTION 17**
What are banks required to do under the Gramm-Leach-Bliley Act (GLBA)?

A. Conduct annual consumer surveys regarding satisfaction with user preferences
B. Process requests for changes to user preferences within a designated time frame
C. Provide consumers with the opportunity to opt out of

receiving telemarketing phone calls
Offer an Opt-Out before transferring PI to an unaffiliated third party for the latter's own use

## QUESTION 18
SCENARIO
Please use the following to answer the next question:

Declan has just started a job as a nursing assistant in a radiology department at Woodland Hospital. He has also started a program to become a registered nurse.

Before taking this career path, Declan was vaguely familiar with the Health Insurance Portability and Accountability Act (HIPAA). He now knows that he must help ensure the security of his patients' Protected Health Information (PHI). Therefore, he is thinking carefully about privacy issues.

On the morning of his first day, Declan noticed that the newly hired receptionist handed each patient a HIPAA privacy notice. He wondered if it was necessary to give these privacy notices to returning patients, and if the radiology department could reduce paper waste through a system of one-time distribution.

He was also curious about the hospital's use of a billing company. He questioned whether the hospital was doing all it could to protect the privacy of its patients if the billing company had details about patients' care.

On his first day Declan became familiar with all areas of the hospital's large radiology department. As he was organizing equipment left in the halfway, he overheard a conversation between two hospital administrators. He was surprised to hear that a portable hard drive containing non-encrypted patient information was missing. The administrators expressed relief that the hospital would be able to avoid liability. Declan was surprised, and wondered whether the hospital had plans to properly report what had happened.

Despite Declan's concern about this issue, he was amazed by the hospital's effort to integrate Electronic Health Records (EHRs) into the everyday care of patients. He thought about the potential for streamlining care even more if they were accessible to all medical facilities nationwide.

Declan had many positive interactions with patients. At the end of his first day, he spoke to one patient, John, whose father had just been diagnosed with a degenerative muscular disease. John was about to get blood work done, and he feared that the blood work could reveal a genetic predisposition to the disease that could affect his ability to obtain insurance coverage. Declan told John that he did not think that was possible, but the patient was wheeled away before he could explain why. John plans to ask a colleague about this.

In one month, Declan has a paper due for one his classes on a health topic of his choice. By then, he will have had many interactions with patients he can use as examples. He will be pleased to give credit to John by name for inspiring him to think more carefully about genetic testing.

Although Declan's day ended with many questions, he was pleased about his new position.

What is the **most likely** way that Declan might directly violate the Health Insurance Portability and Accountability Act (HIPAA)?

A. By being present when patients are checking in
B. By speaking to a patient without prior authorization
C. By ignoring the conversation about a potential breach
By following through with his plans for his upcoming paper

## QUESTION 19
SCENARIO
Please use the following to answer the next question:

Declan has just started a job as a nursing assistant in a radiology department at Woodland Hospital. He has also started a program to become a registered nurse.

Before taking this career path, Declan was vaguely familiar with the Health Insurance Portability and Accountability Act (HIPAA). He now knows that he must help ensure the security of his patients' Protected Health Information (PHI). Therefore, he is thinking carefully about privacy issues.

On the morning of his first day, Declan noticed that the newly hired receptionist handed each patient a HIPAA privacy notice. He wondered if it was necessary to give these privacy notices to returning patients, and if the radiology department could reduce paper waste through a system of one-time distribution.

He was also curious about the hospital's use of a billing company. He questioned whether the hospital was doing all it could to protect the privacy of its patients if the billing company had details about patients' care.

On his first day Declan became familiar with all areas of the hospital's large radiology department. As he was organizing equipment left in the halfway, he overheard a conversation between two hospital administrators. He was surprised to hear that a portable hard drive containing non-encrypted patient information was missing. The administrators expressed relief that the hospital would be able to avoid liability. Declan was surprised, and wondered whether the hospital had plans to properly report what had happened.

Despite Declan's concern about this issue, he was amazed by the hospital's effort to integrate Electronic Health Records (EHRs) into the everyday care of patients. He thought about the potential for streamlining care even more if they were accessible to all medical facilities nationwide.

Declan had many positive interactions with patients. At the end of his first day, he spoke to one patient, John, whose father had just been diagnosed with a degenerative muscular disease. John was about to get blood work done, and he feared that the blood work could reveal a genetic predisposition to the disease that could affect his ability to obtain insurance coverage. Declan told John that he did not think that was possible, but the patient was wheeled away before he could explain why. John plans to ask a colleague about this.

In one month, Declan has a paper due for one his classes on a health topic of his choice. By then, he will have had many interactions with patients he can use as examples. He will be pleased to give credit to John by name for inspiring him to think more carefully about genetic testing.

Although Declan's day ended with many questions, he was pleased about his new position.

How can the radiology department address Declan's concern about paper waste and still comply with the Health Insurance Portability and Accountability Act (HIPAA)?

A. State the privacy policy to the patient verbally
B. Post the privacy notice in a prominent location instead
C. Direct patients to the correct area of the hospital website
D. Confirm that patients are given the privacy notice on their first visit

## QUESTION 20
SCENARIO
Please use the following to answer the next question:

Declan has just started a job as a nursing assistant in a radiology department at Woodland Hospital. He has also started a program to become a registered nurse.

Before taking this career path, Declan was vaguely familiar with the Health Insurance Portability and Accountability Act (HIPAA). He now knows that he must help ensure the security of his patients' Protected Health Information (PHI). Therefore, he is thinking carefully about privacy issues.

On the morning of his first day, Declan noticed that the newly hired receptionist handed each patient a HIPAA privacy notice. He wondered if it was necessary to give these privacy notices to returning patients, and if the radiology department could reduce paper waste through a system of one-time distribution.

He was also curious about the hospital's use of a billing company. He questioned whether the hospital was doing all it could to protect the privacy of its patients if the billing company had details about patients' care.

On his first day Declan became familiar with all areas of the hospital's large radiology department. As he was organizing equipment left in the halfway, he overheard a conversation between two hospital administrators. He was surprised to hear that a portable hard drive containing non-encrypted patient information was missing. The administrators expressed relief that the hospital would be able to avoid liability. Declan was surprised, and wondered whether the hospital had plans to properly report what had happened.

Despite Declan's concern about this issue, he was amazed by the hospital's effort to integrate Electronic Health Records (EHRs) into the everyday care of patients. He thought about the potential for streamlining care even more if they were accessible to all medical facilities nationwide.

Declan had many positive interactions with patients. At the end of his first day, he spoke to one patient, John, whose father had just been diagnosed with a degenerative muscular disease. John was about to get blood work done, and he feared that the blood work could reveal a genetic predisposition to the disease that could affect his ability to obtain insurance coverage. Declan told John that he did not think that was possible, but the patient was wheeled away before he could explain why. John plans to ask a colleague about this.

In one month, Declan has a paper due for one his classes on a health topic of his choice. By then, he will have had many interactions with patients he can use as examples. He will be pleased to give credit to John by name for inspiring him to think more carefully about genetic testing.

Although Declan's day ended with many questions, he was pleased about his new position.

Based on the scenario, what is the **most likely** way Declan's supervisor would answer his question about the hospital's use of a billing company?

A. By suggesting that Declan look at the hospital's publicly posted privacy policy
B. By assuring Declan that third parties are prevented from seeing Private Health Information (PHI)
C. By pointing out that contracts are in place to help ensure the observance of minimum security standards
D. By describing how the billing system is integrated into the hospital's electronic health records (EHR) system

## QUESTION 21
Which entities must comply with the Telemarketing Sales Rule?

A. For-profit organizations and for-profit telefunders regarding charitable solicitations
B. Nonprofit organizations calling on their own behalf
C. For-profit organizations calling businesses when a binding contract exists between them
D. For-profit and not-for-profit organizations when selling additional services to establish customers


## QUESTION 22
Under the Telemarketing Sales Rule, what characteristics of consent must be in place for an organization to acquire an exception to the Do-Not-Call rules for a particular consumer?

A. The consent must be in writing, must state the times when calls can be made to the consumer and must be signed
B. The consent must be in writing, must contain the number to which calls can be made and must have an end date
C. The consent must be in writing, must contain the number to which calls can be made and must be signed
D. The consent must be in writing, must have an end data and must state the times when calls can be made


## QUESTION 23
When does the Telemarketing Sales Rule require an entity to share a do-not-call request across its organization?

A. When the operational structures of its divisions are not transparent
B. When the goods and services sold by its divisions are very similar

C. When a call is not the result of an error or other unforeseen cause
D. When the entity manages user preferences through multiple platforms

**QUESTION 24**
A student has left high school and is attending a public postsecondary institution. Under what condition may a school legally disclose educational records to the parents of the student without consent?

A. If the student has not yet turned 18 years of age
B. If the student is in danger of academic suspension
C. If the student is still a dependent for tax purposes
D. If the student has applied to transfer to another institution

**QUESTION 25**
Which act violates the Family Educational Rights and Privacy Act of 1974 (FERPA)?

A. A K-12 assessment vendor obtains a student's signed essay about her hometown from her school to use as an exemplar for public release
B. A university posts a public student directory that includes names, hometowns, e-mail addresses, and majors
C. A newspaper prints the names, grade levels, and hometowns of students who made the quarterly honor roll
D. University police provide an arrest report to a student's hometown police, who suspect him of a similar crime

**QUESTION 26**
According to FERPA, when can a school disclose records **without** a student's consent?

A. If the disclosure is not to be conducted through email to the third party
B. If the disclosure would not reveal a student's student identification number
C. If the disclosure is to practitioners who are involved in a student's health care
D. If the disclosure is to provide transcripts to a school where a student intends to enroll

## QUESTION 27
What is the **main** purpose of the CAN-SPAM Act?

A. To diminish the use of electronic messages to send sexually explicit materials
B. To authorize the states to enforce federal privacy laws for electronic marketing
C. To empower the FTC to create rules for messages containing sexually explicit content
D. To ensure that organizations respect individual rights when using electronic advertising

## QUESTION 28
The Video Privacy Protection Act of 1988 restricted which of the following?

A. Which purchase records of audio visual materials may be disclosed
B. When downloading of copyrighted audio visual materials is allowed
C. When a user's viewing of online video content can be monitored
D. Who advertisements for videos and video games may target

## QUESTION 29
SCENARIO
Please use the following to answer the next question:

You are the chief privacy officer at HealthCo, a major hospital in a large U.S. city in state A. HealthCo is a HIPAA-covered entity that provides healthcare services to more than 100,000 patients. A third-party cloud computing service provider, CloudHealth, stores and manages the electronic protected health information (ePHI) of these individuals on behalf of HealthCo. CloudHealth stores the data in state B. As part of HealthCo's business associate agreement (BAA) with CloudHealth, HealthCo requires CloudHealth to implement security measures, including industry standard encryption practices, to adequately protect the data. However, HealthCo did not perform due diligence on CloudHealth before entering the contract, and has not conducted audits of CloudHealth's security measures.

A CloudHealth employee has recently become the victim of a phishing attack. When the employee unintentionally clicked on a link from a suspicious email, the PHI of more than 10,000 HealthCo patients was compromised. It has since been published online. The HealthCo cybersecurity team quickly identifies the perpetrator as a known hacker who has launched similar attacks on other hospitals – ones that exposed the PHI of public figures including celebrities and politicians.

During the course of its investigation, HealthCo discovers that CloudHealth has not encrypted the PHI in accordance with the terms of its contract. In addition, CloudHealth has not provided privacy or security training to its employees. Law enforcement has requested that HealthCo provide its investigative report of the

breach and a copy of the PHI of the individuals affected.

A patient affected by the breach then sues HealthCo, claiming that the company did not adequately protect the individual's ePHI, and that he has suffered substantial harm as a result of the exposed data. The patient's attorney has submitted a discovery request for the ePHI exposed in the breach.

What is the **most** significant reason that the U.S. Department of Health and Human Services (HHS) might impose a penalty on HealthCo?

A. Because HealthCo did not require CloudHealth to implement appropriate physical and administrative measures to safeguard the ePHI
B. Because HealthCo did not conduct due diligence to verify or monitor CloudHealth's security measures
C. Because HIPAA requires the imposition of a fine if a data breach of this magnitude has occurred
D. Because CloudHealth violated its contract with HealthCo by not encrypting the ePHI

**QUESTION 30**
Which of the following types of information would an organization generally **NOT** be required to disclose to law enforcement?

A. Information about medication errors under the Food, Drug and Cosmetic Act
B. Money laundering information under the Bank Secrecy Act of 1970
C. Information about workspace injuries under OSHA requirements
D. Personal health information under the HIPAA Privacy Rule

## QUESTION 31

A law enforcement subpoenas the ACME telecommunications company for access to text message records of a person suspected of planning a terrorist attack. The company had previously encrypted its text message records so that only the suspect could access this data.

What law did ACME violate by designing the service to prevent access to the information by a law enforcement agency?

A. SCA
B. ECPA
C. CALEA
D. USA Freedom Act

## QUESTION 32

What practice do courts commonly require in order to protect certain personal information on documents, whether paper or electronic, that is involved in litigation?

A. Redaction
B. Encryption
C. Deletion
D. Hashing

## QUESTION 33

What is an exception to the Electronic Communications Privacy Act of 1986 ban on interception of wire, oral and electronic communications?

A. Where one of the parties has given consent
B. Where state law permits such interception
C. If an organization intercepts an employee's purely personal call
D. Only if all parties have given consent

**QUESTION 34**
What practice does the USA FREEDOM Act **NOT** authorize?

A. Emergency exceptions that allows the government to target roamers
B. An increase in the maximum penalty for material support to terrorism
C. An extension of the expiration for roving wiretaps
D. The bulk collection of telephone data and internet metadata

**QUESTION 35**
The rules for "e-discovery" **mainly** prevent which of the following?

A. A conflict between business practice and technological safeguards
B. The loss of information due to poor data retention practices
C. The practice of employees using personal devices for work
D. A breach of an organization's data retention program

**QUESTION 36**
What do the Civil Rights Act, Pregnancy Discrimination Act, Americans with Disabilities Act, Age Discrimination Act, and Equal Pay Act all have in common?

A. They require employers not to discriminate against certain classes when employees use personal information
B. They require that employers provide reasonable accommodations to certain classes of employees
C. They afford certain classes of employees' privacy

protection by limiting inquiries concerning their personal information
D. They permit employers to use or disclose personal information specifically about employees who are members of certain classes

## QUESTION 37
SCENARIO
Please use the following to answer the next question:

Larry has become increasingly dissatisfied with his telemarketing position at SunriseLynx, and particularly with his supervisor, Evan. Just last week, he overheard Evan mocking the state's Do Not Call list, as well as the people on it. "If they were really serious about not being bothered," Evan said, "They'd be on the national DNC list. That's the only one we're required to follow. At SunriseLynx, we call until they ask us not to."

Bizarrely, Evan requires telemarketers to keep records of recipients who ask them to call "another time." This, to Larry, is a clear indication that they don't want to be called at all. Evan doesn't see it that way.

Larry believes that Evan's arrogance also affects the way he treats employees. The U.S. Constitution protects American workers, and Larry believes that the rights of those at SunriseLynx are violated regularly. At first Evan seemed friendly, even connecting with employees on social media. However, following Evan's political posts, it became clear to Larry that employees with similar affiliations were the only ones offered promotions.

Further, Larry occasionally has packages containing personal-use items mailed to work. Several times, these have come to him already opened, even though this name was clearly marked. Larry thinks the opening of personal mail is common at SunriseLynx, and that Fourth

Amendment rights are being trampled under Evan's leadership.

Larry has also been dismayed to overhear discussions about his coworker, Sadie. Telemarketing calls are regularly recorded for quality assurance, and although Sadie is always professional during business, her personal conversations sometimes contain sexual comments. This too is something Larry has heard Evan laughing about. When he mentioned this to a coworker, his concern was met with a shrug. It was the coworker's belief that employees agreed to be monitored when they signed on. Although personal devices are left alone, phone calls, emails and browsing histories are all subject to surveillance. In fact, Larry knows of one case in which an employee was fired after an undercover investigation by an outside firm turned up evidence of misconduct. Although the employee may have stolen from the company, Evan could have simply contacted the authorities when he first suspected something amiss.

Larry wants to take action, but is uncertain how to proceed.

In what area does Larry have a misconception about private-sector employee rights?

A. The applicability of federal law
B. The enforceability of local law
C. The strict nature of state law
D. The definition of tort law

## QUESTION 38
SCENARIO
Please use the following to answer the next question:

Larry has become increasingly dissatisfied with his telemarketing position at SunriseLynx, and particularly with his supervisor, Evan. Just last week, he overheard Evan mocking the state's Do Not Call list, as well as the people on it. "If they were really serious about not being bothered," Evan said, "They'd be on the national DNC list. That's the only one we're required to follow. At SunriseLynx, we call until they ask us not to."

Bizarrely, Evan requires telemarketers to keep records of recipients who ask them to call "another time." This, to Larry, is a clear indication that they don't want to be called at all. Evan doesn't see it that way.

Larry believes that Evan's arrogance also affects the way he treats employees. The U.S. Constitution protects American workers, and Larry believes that the rights of those at SunriseLynx are violated regularly. At first Evan seemed friendly, even connecting with employees on social media. However, following Evan's political posts, it became clear to Larry that employees with similar affiliations were the only ones offered promotions.

Further, Larry occasionally has packages containing personal-use items mailed to work. Several times, these have come to him already opened, even though this name was clearly marked. Larry thinks the opening of personal mail is common at SunriseLynx, and that Fourth Amendment rights are being trampled under Evan's leadership.

Larry has also been dismayed to overhear discussions about his coworker, Sadie. Telemarketing calls are regularly recorded for quality assurance, and although Sadie is always professional during business, her personal conversations sometimes contain sexual comments. This too is something Larry has heard Evan laughing about. When he mentioned this to a coworker, his concern was met with a shrug. It was the coworker's belief that employees agreed to be monitored when they signed on. Although personal devices are left alone, phone calls, emails and browsing histories are all subject to surveillance.

In fact, Larry knows of one case in which an employee was fired after an undercover investigation by an outside firm turned up evidence of misconduct. Although the employee may have stolen from the company, Evan could have simply contacted the authorities when he first suspected something amiss.

Larry wants to take action, but is uncertain how to proceed.

Which act would authorize Evan's undercover investigation?

A. The Whistleblower Protection Act
B. The Stored Communications Act (SCA)
C. The National Labor Relations Act (NLRA)
D. The Fair and Accurate Credit Transactions Act (FACTA)

**QUESTION 39**
Which of the following is **most likely** to provide privacy protection to private-sector employees in the United States?

A. State law, contract law, and tort law
B. The Federal Trade Commission Act (FTC Act)
C. Amendments one, four, and five of the U.S. Constitution
D. The U.S. Department of Health and Human Services (HHS)

**QUESTION 40**
What role does the U.S. Constitution play in the area of workplace privacy?

A. It provides enforcement resources to large employers, but not to small businesses

B. It provides legal precedent for physical information security, but not for electronic security
C. It provides contractual protections to members of labor unions, but not to employees at will
D. It provides significant protections to federal and state governments, but not to private-sector employment

## QUESTION 41
Which federal act does **NOT** contain provisions for preempting stricter state laws?

A. The CAN-SPAM Act
B. The Children's Online Privacy Protection Act (COPPA)
C. The Fair and Accurate Credit Transactions Act (FACTA)
D. The Telemarketing Consumer Protection and Fraud Prevention Act

## QUESTION 42
Which of the following is commonly required for an entity to be subject to breach notification requirements under most state laws?

A. The entity must conduct business in the state
B. The entity must have employees in the state
C. The entity must be registered in the state
D. The entity must be an information broker

## QUESTION 43
What is the **most likely** reason that states have adopted their own data breach notification laws?

A. Many states have unique types of businesses that require specific legislation

B. Many lawmakers believe that federal enforcement of current laws has not been effective
C. Many types of organizations are not currently subject to federal laws regarding breaches
D. Many large businesses have intentionally breached the personal information of their customers

**QUESTION 44**
Which federal law or regulation preempts state law?

A. Health Insurance Portability and Accountability Act
B. Controlling the Assault of Non-Solicited Pornography and Marketing Act
C. Telemarketing Sales Rule
D. Electronic Communications Privacy Act of 1986

**QUESTION 45**
California's SB 1386 was the **first** law of its type in the United States to do what?

A. Require commercial entities to disclose a security data breach concerning personal information about the state's residents
B. Require notification of non-California residents of a breach that occurred in California
C. Require encryption of sensitive information stored on servers that are Internet connected
D. Require state attorney general enforcement of federal regulations against unfair and deceptive trade practices

## QUESTION 46
Most states with data breach notification laws indicate that notice to affected individuals must be sent in the "most expeditious time possible without unreasonable delay." By contrast, which of the following states currently imposes a definite limit for notification to affected individuals?

A. Maine
B. Florida
C. New York
D. California

## QUESTION 47
Which of the following is **NOT** a principle found in the APEC Privacy Framework?

A. Integrity of Personal Information.
B. Access and Correction.
C. Preventing Harm.
D. Privacy by Design.

## QUESTION 48
Federal laws establish which of the following requirements for collecting personal information of minors under the age of 13?

A. Implied consent from a minor's parent or guardian, or affirmative consent from the minor.
B. Affirmative consent from a minor's parent or guardian before collecting the minor's personal information online.
C. Implied consent from a minor's parent or guardian before collecting a minor's personal information online, such as when they permit the minor to use the internet.

D. Affirmative consent of a parent or guardian before collecting personal information of a minor offline (e.g., in person), which also satisfies any requirements for online consent.

## QUESTION 49

If an organization maintains data classified as high sensitivity in the same system as data classified as low sensitivity, which of the following is the **most likely** outcome?

A. The organization will still be in compliance with most sector-specific privacy and security laws.
B. The impact of an organizational data breach will be more severe than if the data had been segregated.
C. Temporary employees will be able to find the data necessary to fulfill their responsibilities.
D. The organization will be able to address legal discovery requests efficiently without producing more information than necessary.

## QUESTION 50

Which of the following **best** describes the ASIA-Pacific Economic Cooperation (APEC) principles?

A. A bill of rights for individuals seeking access to their personal information.
B. A code of responsibilities for medical establishments to uphold privacy laws.
C. An international court ruling on personal information held in the commercial sector.
D. A baseline of marketers' minimum responsibilities for providing opt-out mechanisms.

## QUESTION 51

Which of the following became the **first** state to pass a law specifically regulating the practices of data brokers?

A. Washington.
B. California.
C. New York.
D. Vermont.

## QUESTION 52

Acme Student Loan Company has developed an artificial intelligence algorithm that determines whether an individual is likely to pay their bill or default. A person who is determined by the algorithm to be more likely to default will receive frequent payment reminder calls, while those who are less likely to default will not receive payment reminders.

Which of the following **most accurately** reflects the privacy concerns with Acme Student Loan Company using artificial intelligence in this manner?

A. If the algorithm uses risk factors that impact the automatic decision engine. Acme must ensure that the algorithm does not have a disparate impact on protected classes in the output.
B. If the algorithm makes automated decisions based on risk factors and public information, Acme need not determine if the algorithm has a disparate impact on protected classes.
C. If the algorithm's methodology is disclosed to consumers, then it is acceptable for Acme to have a disparate impact on protected classes.
D. If the algorithm uses information about protected classes to make automated decisions, Acme must ensure that the algorithm does not have a disparate impact on protected classes in the output.

## QUESTION 53

Global Manufacturing Co's Human Resources department recently purchased a new software tool. This tool helps evaluate future candidates for executive roles by scanning emails to see what those candidates say and what is said about them. This provides the HR department with an automated "360 review" that lets them

know how the candidate thinks and operates, what their peers and direct reports say about them, and how well they interact with each other. What is the most important step for the Human Resources Department to take when implementing this new software?

A. Making sure that the software does not unintentionally discriminate against protected groups.

B. Ensuring that the software contains a privacy notice explaining that employees have no right to privacy as long as they are running this software on organization systems to scan email systems.

C. Confirming that employees have read and signed the employee handbook where they have been advised that they have no right to privacy as long as they are using the organization's systems, regardless of the protected group or laws enforced by EEOC.

D. Providing notice to employees that their emails will be scanned by the software and creating automated profiles.


## QUESTION 54

What type of material is **exempt** from an individual's right to disclosure under the Privacy Act?

A. Material requires by statute to be maintained and used solely for research purposes.

B. Material reporting investigative efforts to prevent unlawful persecution of an individual.

C. Material used to determine potential collaboration with foreign governments in negotiation of trade deals.

D. Material reporting investigative efforts pertaining to the enforcement of criminal law.

## QUESTION 55
All of the following common law torts are relevant to employee privacy under US law EXCEPT?

A. Infliction of emotional distress.

B. Intrusion upon seclusion.

C. Defamation

D. Conversion.

## QUESTION 56
John, a California resident, receives notification that a major corporation with $500 million in annual revenue has experienced a data breach. John's personal information in their possession has been stolen, including his full name and social security numb. John also learns that the corporation did not have reasonable cybersecurity measures in place to safeguard his personal information.

Which of the following answers **most accurately** reflects John's ability to pursue a legal claim against the corporation under the California Consumer Privacy Act (CCPA)?

A. John has no right to sue the corporation because the CCPA does not address any data breach rights.

B. John cannot sue the corporation for the data breach because only the state's Attoney General has authority to file suit under the CCPA.

C. John can sue the corporation for the data breach but only to recover monetary damages he actually suffered as a

result of the data breach.
D. John can sue the corporation for the data breach to recover monetary damages suffered as a result of the data breach, and in some circumstances seek statutory damages irrespective of whether he suffered any financial harm.

**QUESTION 57**
Sarah lives in San Francisco, California. Based on a dramatic increase in unsolicited commercial emails, Sarah believes that a major social media platform with over 50 million users has collected a lot of personal information about her. The company that runs the platform is based in New York and France.

Why is Sarah entitled to ask the social media platform to delete the personal information they have collected about her?

A. Any company with a presence in Europe must comply with the General Data Protection Regulation globally, including in response to data subject deletion requests.
B. Under Section 5 of the FTC Act, the Federal Trade Commission has held that refusing to delete an individual's personal information upon request constitutes an unfair practice.
C. The California Consumer Privacy Act entitles Sarah to request deletion of her personal information.
D. The New York "Stop Hacks and Improve Electronic Data Security" (SHIELD) Act requires that businesses under New York's jurisdiction must delete customers' personal information upon request.

# Answers

1. **Correct Answer: A**

2. **Correct Answer: B**

3. **Correct Answer: C**
   **Explanation/Reference:**
   Reference:
   https://eits.uga.edu/access_and_security/infosec/pols_regs/policies/dcps/

4. **Correct Answer: B**

5. **Correct Answer: B**

6. **Correct Answer: A**
   **Explanation/Reference:**
   Reference:
   https://en.wikipedia.org/wiki/Global_Privacy_Enforcement_Network

7. **Correct Answer: A**
   **Explanation/Reference:**
   Reference:
   https://www.edweek.org/ew/articles/2014/03/13/26google.h33.html

8. **Correct Answer: B**
   Explanation/Reference:
   Reference:
   https://www.lakesidesoftware.com/sites/default/files/Privacy_Shield_Privacy_Statement.pdf

9. **Correct Answer: D**

10. **Correct Answer: B**

11. **Correct Answer: D**

12. **Correct Answer: D**
    Explanation/Reference:
    Reference:
    https://www.privacyshield.gov/Key-New-Requirements

13. **Correct Answer: D**
    Explanation/Reference:
    Reference:
    https://www.ftc.gov/system/files/2012-31341.pdf

14. **Correct Answer: A**
    Explanation/Reference:
    Reference:
    https://www.healthaffairs.org/do/10.1377/hblog20150304.045199/full/

15. **Correct Answer: D**
    Explanation/Reference:
    Reference:
    https://www.hhs.gov/sites/default/files/RansomwareFa

ctSheet.pdf (page 6)

16. Correct Answer: D
    Explanation/Reference:
    Reference:
    https://www.ftc.gov/enforcement/statutes/fair-accurate-credit-transactions-act-2003

17. Correct Answer: D
    Explanation/Reference:
    Reference:
    https://www.investopedia.com/terms/g/glba.asp

18. Correct Answer: C

19. Correct Answer: C

20. Correct Answer: C

21. Correct Answer: D
    Explanation/Reference:
    Reference:
    https://www.ftc.gov/tips-advice/business-center/guidance/complying-telemarketing-sales-rule

22. Correct Answer: B

23. Correct Answer: C

24. **Correct Answer: C**
    Explanation/Reference:
    Reference:
    https://www2.ed.gov/policy/gen/guid/fpco/pdf/ferpafaq.pdf

25. **Correct Answer: A**

26. **Correct Answer: D**
    Explanation/Reference:
    Reference:
    https://www2.ed.gov/policy/gen/guid/fpco/ferpa/index.html

27. **Correct Answer: D**
    Explanation/Reference:
    Reference:
    https://www.ftc.gov/tips-advice/business-center/guidance/can-spam-act-compliance-guide-business

28. **Correct Answer: A**
    Explanation/Reference:
    Reference:
    https://searchcompliance.techtarget.com/definition/Video-Privacy-Protection-Act-of-1988

29. **Correct Answer: B**

30. **Correct Answer: D**

31. Correct Answer: C
    Explanation/Reference:
    Reference:
    https://www.nap.edu/read/11896/chapter/11#283

32. Correct Answer: A

33. Correct Answer: C
    Explanation/Reference:
    Reference:
    https://www.sciencedirect.com/topics/computer-science/electronic-communications-privacy-act

34. Correct Answer: A
    Explanation/Reference:
    Reference:
    https://www.rand.org/blog/2015/05/the-usa-freedom-act-the-definition-of-a-compromise.html

35. Correct Answer: B

36. Correct Answer: A

37. Correct Answer: A

38. Correct Answer: C

39. Correct Answer: A
    Explanation/Reference:
    Reference:
    https://corporate.findlaw.com/law-library/right-to-privacy-in-the-workplace-in-the-information-age.html

40. Correct Answer: B

41. Correct Answer: D

42. Correct Answer: A

43. Correct Answer: B

44. Correct Answer: A

45. Correct Answer: A
    Explanation/Reference:
    Reference:
    https://corporate.findlaw.com/law-library/california-raises-the-bar-on-data-security-and-privacy.html

46. Correct Answer: B
    Explanation/Reference:
    Reference:
    https://www.itgovernanceusa.com/data-breach-notification-laws

47. **Correct Answer: D**
Explanation/Reference:
Reference:
https://www.google.com/url?sa=t&rct=j&q=&esrc=s&source=web&cd=&ved=2ahUKEwiqtJX4tPHvAhUQG-wKHUoGBgkQFjAHegQIBRAD&url=https%3A%2F%2Fwww.apec.org%2F-%2Fmedia%2FAPEC%2FPublications%2F2016%2F11%2F2016-CTI-Report-to-Ministers%2FTOC%2FAppendix-17-Updates-to-theAPEC-Privacy-Framework.pdf&usg=AOvVaw1Yysi4Ym_1VaCw1VZiB70a

48. **Correct Answer: B**
Explanation/Reference:
Reference:
https://www.ftc.gov/tips-advice/business-center/guidance/complying-coppa-frequently-asked-questions-0

49. **Correct Answer: D**

50. **Correct Answer: A**
Explanation/Reference:
Reference:
http://documents1.worldbank.org/curated/en/751621525705087132/text/WPS8431.txt

51. **Correct Answer: D**
    Explanation/Reference:
    Reference:
    https://www.natlawreview.com/article/ringing-2019-new-state-privacy-and-data-security-laws-impacting-data-brokers-and

52. **Correct Answer: B**
    Explanation/Reference:
    Reference:
    https://www.ftc.gov/news-events/blogs/business-blog/2020/04/using-artificial-intelligence-algorithms

53. **Correct Answer: A**
    Explanation/Reference:
    Reference:
    https://www.beckage.com/tag/artificial-intelligence/

54. **Correct Answer: C**

55. **Correct Answer: B**
    Explanation/Reference:
    Reference:
    https://en.wikipedia.org/wiki/Privacy_law

56. **Correct Answer: C**

57. **Correct Answer: C**
    Explanation/Reference:
    Reference:
    https://www.varonis.com/blog/ccpa-vs-gdpr/

www.ingramcontent.com/pod-product-compliance
Lightning Source LLC
Chambersburg PA
CBHW081102240526
45465CB00026B/3272